30 Days of Anime
Color a Page a Day

Mei Yu
Artist on YouTube
Over **450** Million Views

Welcome to Your
30-Day Creative Journey!

Feel your creativity take flight
as you color a page a day.

Color as much or as little of
each page as you like.
You're in control.

When you're done, you'll have 30
proud memories to treasure.

Let's start!

∽ Color a Page a Day! ∽

★ Fun 30-Day Journey!   ★ Build Creativity   ★ Create Memories

★ Feel Accomplished   ★ A Relaxing Hobby - Every Day!

Tips to Use This Book

1. Put a few sheets of paper under the page to help prevent ink from seeping onto the next page.

2. This coloring book works best with markers, pencil crayons, crayons, gel pens, and pens.

3. Try using markers with softer tips. If the tip is very hard, try not to layer colors too many times. Just like with other types of paper, hard tips can scratch the surface if you apply too many layers, or too much pressure. When using alcohol-based or water-based markers, try not to put too much force on the tip. The paper might be ruined, or too much ink might seep through.

4. For pencil crayons, try not to use very sharp tips - they could poke the paper. Angle the tip down so you're coloring more on the side of the tip, rather than at the end point.

5. Before beginning this coloring book, use the Test Area below to try out the art supplies you plan to use. Try varying your pressure, techniques, and types of supplies.

Test Area

Remember to put some blank paper under each page that you're coloring. Enjoy!

This coloring book is dedicated to you!

Relax. Color. Enjoy!

Copyright © 2023 by Mei Yu
Published by Mei Yu Art Inc.

All rights reserved. The use of any part of this publication reproduced, transmitted in any form or by any means, graphic, electronic, mechanical, photocopying, recording, taping, or otherwise, or stored in a retrieval system, without the prior written consent of the author, is an infringement of the copyright law. This book or any part of it is for personal use only. Any commercial use is strictly forbidden.

30 Days of Anime: Color a Page a Day
Paperback ISBN: 978-1-998165-00-1
First Published July 2023
Book design, cover design, text, and illustrations by Mei Yu.
For business inquiries, please contact the author.

This book is custom printed just for you!

100+ Books:
Mei Yu's Book Store
amazon.com/shop/MeiYu

★ All books are made and printed in your closest geographical area.

For example, if you order from the US, it's made in the US.

This book is **100%** hand-drawn by Mei Yu. No A.I. was used in the making of this book.

The Apple logo and iBooks are trademarks of Apple Inc., registered in the U.S. and other countries. App Store is a service mark of Apple Inc. Amazon, Kindle, and all related logos are trademarks of Amazon.com, Inc. or its affiliates.
Android is a trademark of Google LLC.

Day 1

Let's begin this 30-day journey!

By the end, you'll have a
great collection of memories
in this book!

Remember to put some copy
paper under each image
you're coloring.

Have fun!

Day 2

Day 3

Day 4

Day 5

Day 6

Day 7

Day 8

Day 9

Day 10

You're one-third of
the way there!

Keep going :)

Day 11

Day 12

Day 13

Day 14

Day 15

Halfway there!
You can do this.

Day 16

Day 17

Day 18

Day 19

Day 20

Way to go!
Just 10 days left

Day 21

Day 22

Day 23

Day 24

Day 25

Day 26

Day 27

Day 28

Day 29

Day 30

Congratulations
on your gorgeous work!

This book completed by:

_____

on _____ 20____

COMPLETE YOUR SERIES
Have a Relaxing Daily Hobby

100+ Books at:
Mei Yu's Book Store
available at amazon
www.amazon.com/shop/MeiYu

Color a Page a Day!
Feel your creativity SOAR

Mei Yu Book 🔍

Ships to 100+ Countries

COLORING BOOK + ART BOOK IN ONE:

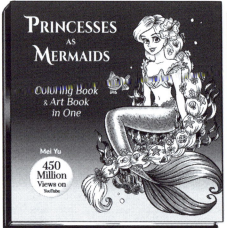
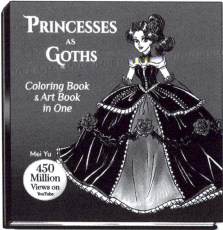
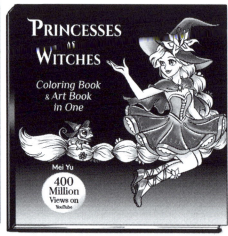

Part Coloring Book, Part Art Book

2 sizes available:
8.5" x 8.5" and 8.5" x 11"

← **Full-color Art** for each design

Lineart to Color → right beside

100+ Books at Mei Yu's Book Store
available at amazon — amazon.com/shop/MeiYu

Start Creating Masterpieces!
Mei Yu Coloring Book 🔍
Ships to 100+ Countries

Unleash your creativity
in Mei Yu's Coloring Books!

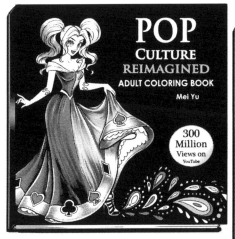

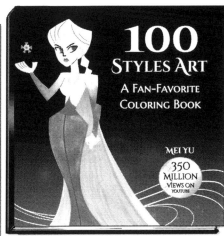
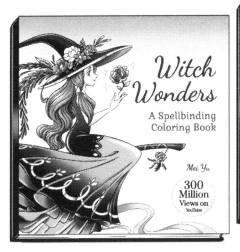

100+ Books at
Mei Yu's Book Store
available at **amazon** amazon.com/shop/MeiYu

Start Creating Masterpieces!

| Mei Yu Coloring Book 🔍 |

Ships to 100+ Countries

More Fan Favorites:

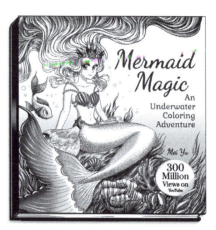
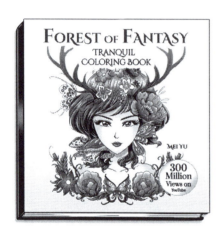
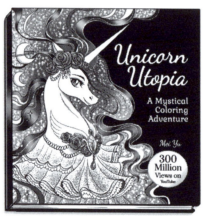

Available in 3 Sizes / Formats:
- Regular Softcover **8.5" x 8.5"**
- Large Softcover **8.5" x 11"**
- Large Hardcover **8.25" x 11"**

Mei Yu's Book Store
available at amazon
www.amazon.com/shop/MeiYu

Start Creating Masterpieces!
Mei Yu Coloring Book 🔍
Ships to 100+ Countries

Complete Your Book Collection:

🖤 **Perfect for** casual colorists, budding artists, + anime / art fans

🖤 **Great with Your** crayons, markers, gel pens, colored pencils

🖤 **Unleash Your** creativity with Inspiring Artwork

🖤 **Own Now or Gift** these Creative Adventures!

Mei Yu's Book Store

available at amazon
www.amazon.com/shop/MeiYu

Start Creating Masterpieces!

[Mei Yu 🔍]

Ships to 100+ Countries

Other Paperbacks (Full Color)

How to Draw Books

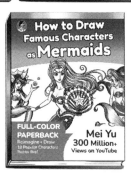

Art Book

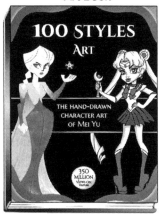

Draw Quick + Easy

(Black/White Paperbacks)

Mei Yu's Book Store

available at www.amazon.com/shop/MeiYu

Mei Yu 🔍

Ships to 100+ Countries

Mei Yu's How to Draw eBooks

★ DRAW 1 IN 20 SERIES

AND MORE...

★ Draw Reimagined Characters Series

AND MORE...

Learn Skills - Create Your Own Characters!

 https://itunes.apple.com/us/author/mei-yu/id1055789735

available at **amazon** www.amazon.com/shop/MeiYu

Android users: Download the Kindle App to get my eBooks
Kobo users: Search "Mei Yu Art" in the Kobo app or Kobo website

Search Amazon, Kindle, iTunes, Kobo

★ **Fun2draw™ Series**

   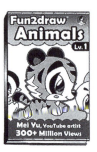  

★ Draw 1 Character in 10 Art Styles

AND MORE...

Complete Your Art Class!

Mei Yu Art 🔍

Search Amazon, Kindle, iTunes, Kobo

Mei Yu's APP

DRAW 50 ANIME MANGA LESSONS

Download Now + Draw Better Today!

https://apps.apple.com/developer/mei-yu/id674269351

Mei Yu 🔍

About Mei Yu

Mei Yu started drawing on walls at age 2. She self-taught herself how to draw until high school. In her graduating year, Mei won 17 local and national art awards and scholarships in Canada. After graduating from college, she designed for animated shows in Vancouver. She lives in Canada.

Since 2004, Mei has been teaching kids and teens her popular anime and cartoon lessons in schools and libraries in Vancouver. Mei continues to inform, entertain, and inspire millions around the world on her popular art channel on YouTube at **youtube.com/MeiYu** with over 1.5 million subscribers, 1000 videos, and 450 million views.

Now, Mei uses her 30+ years of art experience to help more kids, teens, and aspiring artists with her hundreds of well-loved coloring books, how to draw books, and art books with the help of her brother. Many parents, teachers, and librarians have told Mei they love her beautiful artwork, positive attitude, and cheerful personality.

Mei working on her "100 Paint" video for her fans.

Many of Mei's fans have told her she has ignited their passion for art and creativity. Some were inspired to start drawing for the very first time, while others went back to their art journeys.

Other fans are furthering their art education and pursuing their dreams in art, comics, fashion, and design. Some of Mei's earliest fans have now become artists.

Mei is constantly creating more books, eBooks, and other projects to help inspire more people around the world.

Visit her at:
meiyuart.com

Printed in Poland
by Amazon Fulfillment
Poland Sp. z o.o., Wrocław